P9-AGI-882

STAINED GLASS

WITHDRAWN
UTSA LIBRARIES

WORKS BY WILLIAM MILLS

Watch for the Fox

The Stillness in Moving Things:
  The World of Howard Nemerov

I Know a Place

Introduction to *Louisiana Cajuns*

STAINED GLASS

Poems by William Mills

LOUISIANA STATE UNIVERSITY PRESS

Baton Rouge and London   *1979*

Copyright © 1979 by William Mills
All rights reserved
Manufactured in the United States of America

Some of the poems published here have previously appeared
in *Southern Review*, *New Orleans Review*, *Mississippi Review*,
The Back Door, and *Quarterly West*.

Design: Dwight Agner
Typeface: VIP Bembo
Composition: LSU Press
Printing and binding: Thomson-Shore, Inc.

LIBRARY OF CONGRESS CATALOGING IN PUBLICATION DATA

Mills, William, 1935–
    Stained glass: poems.
    I. Title.
PS3563.I4234S7   811'.5'4   78–11893
ISBN 0–8071–0488–4
ISBN 0–8071–0489–2 pbk.

LIBRARY
The University of Texas
At San Antonio

Publication of this book has been supported by a grant from the
National Endowment for the Arts in Washington, D.C., a federal
agency.

For my mother and father

CONTENTS

STAINED GLASS

STARLIGHT
IN ARKANSAS

Starlight in Arkansas
Some would say
Is no different from starlight
Anywhere.

This light beyond our bed
Will be remembered by us
Only in this conjunction.

No one in Yemen or Mexico
Will ever know it like this.

They wouldn't even
If they came to Arkansas.

BEGINNINGS

What is vouchsafed
  For the journey
Is mostly unclear,
  A series of guesses,
Rebuttals, silences.

The dialogue with nature
  Begins more and more
To seem like an echo
  Of our voices.

Relations
  Between numbers
Get Gödel's grin.

Even with us,
  Two nudes in a bed,
Our structure rests
  On an earlier proposition.

What holds our twin fires
  Together?
A black body from which we race,
  Or the black gravity
Of our last big bang?

A PHILOSOPHICAL EVENING
IN LOUISIANA
for Albert Waterson

In my neighbor's field
I have watched
Through the long afternoon
A white egret
Make his way from flight
To chained, slow death.

The old woman who owns the field
Owns the pond
Owns some mallards in the pond.

Each spring, audacious, cunning crows
Make their move
As the eggs are laid.
Precisely.
Other seasons their black flights
Seem random to us,
Their isolated remarks
Most notable in quiet winter skies.
Spring focuses their lives
And then the woman
Sets her traps
Atop long poles where the crows
Light to check things out.

She catches many cattle egrets
Who have no taste for mallard eggs,
But rather like to walk
Stately beside the cows
Looking for ticks.

The redneck crone
Raised the mallards from eggs
And keeps their wings clipped
("civilizing" them so to speak,
   as they race the bank
   believing they can take off,
   all this from memories).
She likes to eat mallards.
Precisely.

The mallards feed in the pond,
The crows on eggs and ducklings
And the white egrets,
Well, they don't fit this chain,
Precisely.

Lately some friends have questioned
Matters of traps
And even of eating mallard ducks.
Vegetables and fruits would have the day—
Another chain, but one that can't call out,
Though the plants came first
And without their breath
No animals, no doubt.

This trap upon the pole
Is no precipice in the Indian Caucasus,
The egret no Prometheus—
For its white fire
Has been stolen by the crone
Who was looking for crows,
The crone hungry for mallard meat.

4

There seem some contradictions here.
Yet surely laughter
Will not resolve them
To any decent unity,
These opposites of mallards and crows,
Egrets and old women with their traps.

These elements simply must remain
Held in the mind
Till it too is eaten up.

LOUISIANA NIGHT

A man has to watch himself very
   carefully
When late at night
   he lies alone and listens,
And the cicadas
   suddenly
Stop.

THE WOUND BECOMES
A WEAPON

Lying here in the rat dawn
When the bar sounds in the street
Have said their goodbyes
And go from the earth
As quick as whores
Who didn't get their price
My heart shifts suddenly
Like ice cubes in a tall forgotten drink
And over and over
I consider the wound I gave you,
The wound which became a weapon.
Soon you, too, narrowed to a sound
On the stairs below.
I stare at your shoes.
Tomorrow the bar sounds return.

7

SATURDAY

A cold front is moving in
Whose last stop
Before Arkansas
Is Missouri.
You accept all of this with grace
Because before your eyes
There is a light;
Before your eyes
A young woman half tight
And there is music.

The leaves this year
Didn't fall with red-orange glory,
The rain held itself
To Florida, or a hoary
Sea that didn't need it.

Chance has no dinner coat,
Eats hurriedly.

So let this Sunday go,
Think about tonight.
The pressure is building
From the front in Missouri,
I am forty and will cover up,
Look to the woman
Look to the light
Expect the cold.

A VOTE
FOR JANUARY

It is very important
To make a record
Someplace
Every chance—
Like on this clear winter afternoon
When the woods
Are dry and
The frogs and cicadas
Do not seem ominous
But voices
That want to affront death.

Thus, being no dancer
Or man with paints,
I go on record
For a clear winter day—
Against a later time
When the woods
Turn to swamps,
And death taunts
Are empty threats.

MOTEL

This motel room
On Interstate 40 West
Has one copy of a blue bird,
One lamp, one chair.

Events have fallen out
That no one knows
I am lying here
Watching the major league
In this single bed.

For some reason
(Maybe the color blue)
I remember another scene—
This one on a box of salt,
The one with the girl
Who shields herself from the rain
And salts the ground behind her
With salt from a box with a girl
Who shields herself from the rain
And salts the ground behind,
And on and on,
Laying waste to the land
None of them looking back.

FOR VIRGINIA,
WHO WANTED LIMITS

This night train from Leningrad has stopped.
Soviet border guards come through again.
Awake now, the snow of Finland
Beckoning like a white angel,
I think of you in Vilnius
Roaming the cobbled streets,
In love with your father's town.
Chicago-born yourself and terrified
By that beery bustle
That fertile freedom to fail,
You came to Vilnius to learn—
And discovered limits.
American-born myself we came together
In rough play, you lover of Lenin and Lithuania,
Me of limits too, but not by strangers.
Virginia, our ghosts
Have different cradles, different homes.
Mine is my simulacrum, me alone.

THE CALLING

Now this pine-whistled poet
Is on a night train from Moscow to Vilnius.

Clank lurch and steam
Rattle and dream

The ghost of beginning brought him
Out of the red-glancing light

Of Mississippi hills
Into this land of Tsars and commisars.

There are many beginnings.
This one will do.

He has stumbled until now
But he is in Russia.

Clearly he is to be reckoned with
Because even Breshnev worries

What the poets will say. The poet is
Now on the night train to Vilnius.

Clank lurch and steam
Rattle and dream

He cannot speak Russian but
Train hostesses help him.

Laughing together in the rocking car
They exchange the words they know.

They take him to the dining car
Working on a five-year plan

To get him food. He takes
A Lithuanian wine that is strong.

It goes with the soup and stew.
He will make it to Vilnius, he thinks.

Uncovered by their care
He shows a book of his poems

To the railroad hostesses. Expressions
Change fast. He still didn't understand

How poets were thought of here.
They take the book away for a long time

And then the blond who tends the charcoal samovar
Tells him, "I like poetry very much."

He smiles as large as he can.
She brings him hot plum tea.

He believes it is special. He begins to know
The importance and danger of what he does.

Clank lurch and steam
Rattle and dream

Pine-whistled. Red-glancing light.
To Vilnius in the snow. Plum tea.

After many years he receives the call.

RORSCHACH
for Helen Elde

I fly out of Helsinki
In this early light
The ground drops away
Or I drop away from the ground.
It is getting more difficult to tell.

The snow, the birches: then you seem to dance
In the winter air,
Your auburn hair almost hiding those three necklaces
You wear you said
To ward off trouble when it comes back.
The charms are from Africa, I think.
I need my own.
Not believing in charms before
My heart falls now before darkness.

Charms: if I had worn them
Would they have warded you off?
I promise you I would have thrown them away.

We took confession from each other,
The last two penitents
In a world gone deaf.

The ground is gone
And I carry you in that place
Where all darkness comes.
What is the meaning of night,
The birches and snow,
Of you standing in the Finnish light?

WINTER STELE

You have decided marrying won't do.
I could have been the many to your one
And you to me. Instead the world darkens to your kiss.
Rather than cross long love's Rubicon
You chose to stay and be quick pleasure's nun.

Now we stand like straight sticks
That add to nothing, never a home,
Now remain like winter stele of an undone spring
Where people come to ritual and ghosts, to beg and atone.
See us, see us stand, alone and alone.

WRAPPING IT UP
IN THE WESTERN DIVISION

Agatha Carter scored tonight
Despite great opposition
From Frank, her husband.

Ted Calloway will be laid up
Following Prudential's annual office games.

Clarence Henderson carried a lot of grief
On four tries and seems to be a comer.

Mrs. Ashton Philips will be greeted
Back in Milwaukee by her husband
After a losing streak
Across the Midwest.
Rumor has it Mrs. Philips
May be traded.

Observers of the Western Division
Have commented that television
Has changed the game radically
In an attempt to speed up the action.

These observers criticize
Recent player independence
With no apparent loyalty to the home club.

Here's a late one just in—
Clarence Henderson has picked up the option
On Mrs. Philips.

And that about winds it up
In the West.

SCIRUS NIGER

He proceeded with what he thought
Was stealth
Coming down out of the tree
Along the trunk.
Then through the grass running
As if his feet were mostly strangers
To the ground,
The theft of food
On his mind.
After the raid
He returned to the leaves
Eating easily,
Time to look around
And feel sly at the quicker way,
Though maybe his back was beginning to ache.

STAINED GLASS

You started with broken pieces
From many places.
Some were red from the war.

The blacks and whites
Came from my Protestant days.

You even found a use for
Large planes of monochromes—
Those long periods
When I wanted nothing
Except to pick my teeth and look outside.

From an old marriage
You took what fragments could be saved.
Of course you added colors of your own.

It was no window at Chartres,
We both knew that.
Still, on certain days
It brought some pleasure.

A fact of stained glass and light:
Stained glass dies at night.

THE FALLING LIGHT

Outside my window
The falling light
Folding within the trees,
Falling within the white
Sheets of snow. November
And you are everywhere
Upon the white land.
I conjure you,
Nude and hot
Across the white crust
Leaving the dark ground
As you pass.

What could be more unbelievable
Than the cold silent landscape?

MAGIC TARGET

Sometimes I imagine
There at the bottom of the hill
He sat still,
Sweat runneling his dusty face,
Puzzling.
What will they do next?
Friends volunteered the chances.
He thought
(Like the clown
Who sits above the water
As we throw at the magic target):
Not knowing exactly when
The fall will come
Is not knowing at all.

Like the clown
Who climbs back up
He moaned at what they came to do,
Sorry they could not stop.

They could not stop
Because they knew
Without the fall
There is no show at all.

REVERENCE

What is finally true about the young,
They want their elders quickly gone;
To make way they must bring them low.
Oh the elders, they know, they know.

WHAT COULD THIS COLD,
WHAT COULD THIS WILDERNESS

In the gaunt, the fleshless night
When you're not here
I think of the world's feast.

What could this cold, what could this wilderness
Promise your body couldn't quench?
Only an old and childish terror, I think,
One those thin desert religions passed on,
Detours along the sun's way.

Yet the sun forks:
Apollo and Dionysus, too,
The light, the grape
All in the world.

I turn my caravan of fears
Toward your almonds and your well
Forgetting this tale of One,
Knowing that feasting and dancing
Rely on two.

TEOTIHUACAN

Start with the community
Around the Pyramid of the Sun
And the Moon,
A largeness
Now called Teotihuacan,
Where no one can remember
Any building's name
Or what it was there for.
The town stands quite
Exposed in the landscape,
No trace of fortification
Has been found.
For those who try to remember
About such things
It remains only
"The place where one becomes a god."

As you come on it now
You feel how many folks lived there together
Knowing each other easy,
"Bring me a loaf of bread
When you come back"—
Things like that.

Tonight in Louisiana
I kissed a woman
Who is dying
Because some cells
Have lost their way,
Dying with the sureness
Of a call from the bank.

SOUTHERN VORTEX

This Louisiana sun
Draws bits and pieces
In a hot focus.
The foreman has sent me off
From the others to chip paint,
And the heat and white shell glare
Of this lonesome tank farm
May have cooked my head to hallucinations,
May be keeping me from
Understanding this vortex:
Green tanks, scraggled trees,
And one woodpecker,
Grinding out the way.

TWO BIRDS,
A COMMON TREE

After the night
We walked together
By a creek
And a high bluff.

Two hawks circled
Nearby alone
When a diligent
Accidental vulture
Swept himself
Across the blue sky.

No matter. This only
Gave the night and the day
Style.

Two birds screamed,
Went to a common tree.

SEVEN RED APPLES

Over her shoulder
Were seven red apples.
He could see them steadily
As he felt her heart beat,
Her breasts.
He felt ungracious
That the apples
Held his attention,
But they detached themselves
As he detached himself.
Noumenal yet luminous
They levitated
(Like Willard the Wizard's
 floating lady on stage).
Cézanne, come here!
How do the apples
Come between him and her?

WEDINGTON WOODS

Waiting for the eleventh hour
I circle the phone booth in my Volkswagen
While the boys at Johnson's Texaco
Wonder if I'm a low budget
Stickup man in a German getaway car.

I wheel and glide to the booth
Of my love's voice.
The lunch hour is less certain than our lust.

For one hour and fifteen minutes
Our love will walk like a thief
In the Wedington leaves.

Christine, honey, I'm coming.
Just let me get the people's car
Up these stony lanes and gullies
Without ripping out my oil pan
And we will be a two-star lunch
In the woods of Wedington.

What tawdry times
We have met in shopping centers
Or the parks of children
And I, like a runner
Who was his own baton,
Leaped to your Chrysler
Landing on the summer hot Naugahyde,
Landing in your arms.

Then we found our wild garden away from home
Where I find you now, Chrysler covered,
Not in Versailles or Vienna
But in Wedington Woods
Where Ozark hunters have brought
Mysteriously to these trails,
Car tires, the Arkansas *Gazette*,
Bedsprings and mattresses
(all on the trail of the white-tailed deer)
Even a commode with its seat
In a broken salute to the world
That has filled it.
Also, my love, a Ford's backseat,
Passion's platform from some old
Chickasaw rite.
How do the seatless Fords take the
Children to church?
How do the drivers explain?

You want to move on
Deeper into the elms and sycamores?
Your cinnamon skin startles the autumn leaves,
We stop, we touch.
You have decided to be late for work.
Christine this hackberry bush will do
For your blouse, your skirt,
Even your hose if you're careful.

You glow bronze in Wedington
Like a Barlach nude I saw once in New Orleans
After coffee in the museum garden.
I turned then just as suddenly
As I turn to you now
Wondering all the time if a squirrel hunter
Squatting sentinel for his rodent supper
Watches us dance here in the October sunlight.

This beats the parking lot of the Dairy Queen.
You are my dairy queen. I am your Ferdinand.
I am your Raleigh, too. Lie down my love
Here on this Sear's T-shirt, these Penney's pants.

Coming down to your hills of certainty
I know this low calorie naked lunch
Is the business world's finest hour.
Onward to production.

O Christine, Christine: forgetfulness in lust
Demands dynasties.
Christine: More of us may join than joy.
Should we forebear?
Christine!

So you take me in another way, me,
The driver of the people's car,
Stickup man who
Casts his seeds on hackberry, mayhaw and Cherokee,
On red maple, sycamore and elm,
Tracks of the deer and armadillo and coon,
Seeds flung now streaming in the wind,
Now on Wedington.

Drying the people's member with your Dior panties
We turn to ceremony and the guttural rites,
We bury them in an armadillo hole,
Pack them with dirt,
Cover them with Wedington leaves.

I dream the armadillo rooting once more
In his old ground, tunneling and struggling
Into the blue Dior panties,
Then brushing the people's seeds
By every bush and bramble in Wedington.
Come spring, our joy rises
Within every rabbit and jay, every grackle and deer,
All of us together in a bestial chorus of sentients,
While in the long nights of the not yet happened,
Puzzled, shy motorists, watchful hunters
Mention quietly to their closest friends
Of seeing an armadillo dressed strangely human
Trudge purposefully through the dark.

Lord, let every seed, no matter how humble,
Illicit or not, be registered
In the archives of the Holy.
For those whose passion must stop short
Let art, pantheon of our humanity,
Keep permanent what the flesh could not.

FOR YOU WHOM I JUST MET

Two snaggled pines
Behind our friend's cottage
Beckoned like a specter's fingers
As we turned away to the sea.
You said—because I wanted you to—
You'd walk along the beach
You looked at every day.

This first evening we boozed
Through introductions and by night
Were tentative, boozy friends.
You changed your shoes,
Hello'd your teenaged daughters
And then we moved together to the sea.
The season's second storm
Dawdled in the Gulf.

On old pilings we began to talk
Obliquely of the ones we loved before
Protecting them with all the honor due them,
All this above the sea sound of the world's breath.

You had reached some peace
I don't know how
And mostly let me rave.
You said you would like to die
In this sea town.

The gulls' cries break the peace.

Only the erupting white caps
Can be seen in this dark.

Let every calm be only an overture
To its own storm
Until we break too
Like white caps in the night.

NURSERY RHYME

One, two, unbuckling my shoes
I think of you undressing
In the lamplight
Both of us full of what we are
About to give away.

Three, four, close the door
And check the lock.
The children, although
They are old enough to know,
Might become confused
To see us as open
As two wounds
Trying to kiss each other well.

Five, six, the sticks are scattered,
The house gone, I've moved my shoes
And shirt to an apartment and undress alone.
The children are with you.

Seven, eight, lay us straight.
Lay me down
So I can see you in the lamplight again.
For if I die before I sleep
The children will be left with an ugly picture
And their classmates will whisper at school.

Nine, ten, let's do it again.

BARE BLACK
LIMBS

There is a certain way
Cold wind blows through
Bare black limbs
Against a gray sky
That lets you know.

CLEANING UP

On this July overcast afternoon
I would like
An ice cream scoop
To reach deep
And scrape clean
The places where old loves
Stick to the edges.
Let me be.

DEAR MR. EPSTEIN:
1955

I know you were
    expecting your daughter
    for the Easter break

However:
    Some of us veterans of the wars
    of our country
    often, for no reason,
    feel strangely and desperately
    alone

And at such times
    we think it is the least
    the citizens can do
    to loan us their daughters
    for the long nights—

She would write you
    but she is fastened to our bed
    which has become, as the
    poets say, everywhere—

She has told me that you were
    never a soldier,
    but that your people
    have suffered a great deal
    during the war before last—

This will be enough I think
    to help you understand.

                    yr new friend,
                        J

SUTRA

It was when you skipped
Or fluttered, old heart,
That you became my Zen master.
You whacked me from behind.
My life runs out with the hourglass sand,
Leaving only an emptiness above
To fill the one below.

THE SOUND
OF HAMMERING

The sky made no sound,
The trees had no wind,
No cars passed.
At once the old terror set in.
The mind wiped clean.

When, O beatitude,
Came the beautiful
Sound of hammering
Across the road.
My neighbor was building
His barn.

AMONG THIS ALL

The book about my betters
In this matter of the stress
And assonance of letters
Held my eye and should,

When I happened to look out
To the thin November snow,
The limestone cliff rutting
The frantic sky.

The rocks against the sky
The trees among the snow,
I stand here modified
By me among this all.

FOX SQUIRREL

Rat, I never thought
I would come to this—
I have been sitting beneath this live oak
For thirty minutes, know your
Memory is not as long as mine.
I know how these sixes will undo your tough hide
With the shock that is briefest and everlasting—
This thinking of you
In the middle of your leap,
Your joy, your red ghost.

THE HUNTER'S SWORD

Curious, I think,
How being slashed earlier this evening
By your look
I would come to stare
At Orion
So far away.
For what?
Is it the axis sickness,
Trying to find that which
All else turns around,
A stillness among the stars?

Despite all the weight
Of Newton's name,
His calculus and contempt
For poetry,
His lust for some body
Absolutely at rest,
All that's gone—
Fixed stars and all.
In a swirl.

I leave one sword for another,
A fixed point
For one that moves,
A sword whose light
Takes a thousand years to touch my eyes
When I saw yours this night.
Why should I wait so long to die?

SIR:

Not believing in you
It is awkward
To bend the knee.
No matter. At such moments
I improvise.

Such a woman
And the summer's gallop
In the midst of the common adversity
Does not by this common man
Go unnoticed.

AT LEAST

I wish
When it comes
There could be
A hazing of the eyes
As warning
Just so the difference
Between is and isn't
Might be given a memorial,
One more picture—
Perhaps some winter oaks
Arterial against an evening sky.

TORNADOES AND
TRAILER PARKS

Like combat, I know the general threat
Of the world's temper is much greater
Than the tornado's narrow whim.
Yet here in this slight metal box
Where I lie hearing the winter rain,
The last ellipsis, the final contraction
Draw me to myself.
Boxed in this overture to the dread rectangle
I consider myself as blown flower and seed,
Here in the deep middle of the world,
World of my trailer, of myself,
Encrusted by the layered past.
Hard as the shell of my deeply buried seed
I pound on the walls and incant the warmer rains.
Fortress I would have you melt,
Fall down, be gone.
The heart of the seed
Wants the burning sun,
The spiteful wind.

COCK

Many mornings
The neighbor's barnyard cacophony
Has served as the final wedge,
Splitting an aching head
Whereupon the halves of the head
Have fallen to the bedroom floor,
Severing the memory of last night's fun.

This morning (the moon gone,
The sun not yet ready to make its move)
My dark was such I couldn't
Find the clock,
Leaving me uncertain hours
With no vouchers for courage,
When a proud young cock's crow
Served notice to the world at large
And his hen house in particular
That sun or not,
Here was his solitary
Announcement to the dark.

MADE IN THE SHADE

Shadows should be gifts to aging lovers.
Their bodies seem what they once were
When unafraid of straightforward light,
Ripe athletes refracted through
Some accidental courtesy.
The bodies together,
(Her rusty nipples, his slack chest)
Become through this courtesy,
This subordination of time's glare,
A retreat to numinous grace.

IN THE
HEART'S MIDNIGHT

In the heart's midnight
When you think the last tock
Has ticked,
Fix your mind quickly
On the window pane,
The way the water
Shimmers down the
Hard membrane,
Or consider
The car passing
With the broken muffler—
Just at that moment
Don't consider time.

GETTING READY
TO GO OUT

It came like a blast from Tannhäuser
Making even this old skeptic
Think Thor was fed up.
3 A.M. was bright as
A welder's arc over water.

The rain drove its way to my bed
My sheet shroud flapped
And I sensed this was turning
Into something different.
Tree branches and trash
Passed me like scared birds
And then that much touted
Locomotive whirred to its next stop.
I got ready to go out.

Later I noticed I didn't turn
To the departed
(God or my divorced wife)
But concentrated on my body
Twisted in the bathroom.

In the morning
I started bitching about
All the cleanup,
The roof tin bent,
The fences crushed,
The cows gone.

ON BEING ASKED TO WRITE
MORE HUMOROUS POETRY
for Les Phillabaum

Hell, I want to.
During the day
Under the clear skies
Of Arkansas autumn
I can move from awe to grin
Like Fred Astaire.

With my friends and cigarettes and beer
We lie and laugh at Roger's Pool Hall
Valhalla of the common spirit
Where no story is false.

But the day threatens rain and
Doesn't. The girl promises love and
Runs away. I watch the dirt
Dancing down,
The dark tapping in again.

SINCE THE BLOND LADY DECIDED
TO LEAVE ME TO LOOK
FOR HER INDIVIDUALITY

The rain is playing its drum
On a morning that could be a black rag
But I am my own interpreter
And so take me blanket-wrapped
On a cold floor
Here in February New Orleans
As a man of good position.

I could take that whirring sound
As death's railroad
But have the presence of mind
To fit it to the green
St. Charles streetcar
As it lurches the boulevards.

When the rain stops
I will, I think,
Scare up a scruffy blue pigeon
In the square
And feed her some corn.
This notwithstanding I do not like
Crowds of pigeons in a city
Shitting on saints' heads.
But wanting to pay
Love and beauty's cartage
I will stand back
To watch.

EQUINOX

With the earth's new tilting
The northern wind slides south.
Summer makes its way
Toward St. Petersburg.
Not prepared for the stranger
I stand naked before the window
And late evening guitars.

We common two
Flash our heat
Before the night
And the day's disasters,
We go in a burst
Of fast fire.
Oh, strumming guitars.

The newspapers persist
About the burning fields
The harvest stolen
But we, steady as the night,
Keep coming home again.
Oh guitars
For the common two.

MY FORGETFUL
HEART

The flower's memory
Is very long,
It rarely opens
Itself in the cold.

Now has become
Winter for me.
My forgetful heart
Opens itself
To your sting
And sting
And sting.

ONCE IS NOT ENOUGH

Just to show you how times change,
She explains to me how the one time
Was fine and all that
But in point of fact
She was used to more
And was this going to be the show.

To which
I began to remember the '30s
When once was not only enough
For any number of affairs
But beat the hell out of
One times nothing
(To get technical).

Part of the chagrin is play.
I know, you know.
But still
I will hold in this old mind
The meaning of *one*.
This meditation
Should take quite a long time.

COMING

Most of us are waiting.
Some are holding off marriage
Until the right one comes.
Others who would have wished
The company of children
On the long march
Have struck an inorganic rhythm
Or else have capped the well.

Pundits must soon decide
If our Athens is now golden
With a faint shadow on the eastern slopes.
In which case as we prepare
For the evening news
We hope the cameraman will
Focus clearly enough on our Macedonian.
For that matter the microphone
Might pick up Demosthenes
Instead of the audio difficulty
We have come to expect.
We wait.

Through our house's window
We stare to find . . . just what?
Will he be on a quiet horse
Like Bolivar or Il Duce,
Or in some shiny open car
Surrounded by running guards?
Will it be from the desert out back
For a much greater event,
That beast coming closer?

THE EXCLUSION
PRINCIPLE

Somewhere in my fortieth year
And a cold Sunday
I try to explain
How the exclusion principle
Has left me with three friends
None in the place where I live.
Childless,
Three degrees and three books,
I, who never could understand hard thoughts,
Fidgit if certainty lasts
Longer than a Methodist sermon,
Am lately preoccupied
With an abandoned topcoat
On a chair's back
In a hotel with wooden floors.

OUR FATHERS AT CORINTH

for William J. Mills, Co. A, 24th Mississippi Infantry Regiment. Died June 18, 1862.
Buried in an unknown soldier's grave, Enterprise, Mississippi

"Let the impending battle decide our fate, and add one
more illustrious page to the history of our Revolution,
one to which our children will turn with noble pride,
saying, 'Our fathers were at the battle of Corinth.'"
                    P. G. T. Beauregard, General, Commanding

Winter in Mississippi and your sons stand before you,
All of us together now, here between Chunky River and
Okatibbe Creek. You lie unmarked in these four hundred
Gray stones, still in formation and like enlisted men
Everywhere mostly unknown. It was this
That haunted your children,
That we didn't even know your name,
Only that you never came home.

The specter of our forgetfulness drove us
To front porches of the old of Greene County
Wanting to put a name to your wraith,
An end to our neglect.
As we rocked our way to eighteen hundred and sixty-two,
A hundred-year-old cousin remembered
You had walked the long way to Corinth.
That your young son got a licking
For trying to follow you.

She also said your name, great-grandfather.
With this we followed you to these cracked stones.

The records showed it to be
A late spring of blood.
You clustered at the courthouse
With your brash and ruddy cousins
Come to watch the lieutenant dressed in gray

56

Come to hear him talk about the fight.
He spoke of April at Shiloh and the butcher's bill,
Of General Johnston dying,
Of Mississippians buried there.
He spoke of Halleck with twice our number
Moving on Corinth.
He read a letter from Jeff Davis:
"Beauregard must have reinforcements . . .
The case of vital importance.
Send forward to Corinth
All the armed men you can furnish."
What parts of the late spring day
Warred in your Anglo-Saxon mind
As you moved slowly from the dock
Of rhythmical certainties in Greene County
To the caesura of war, that pause
As the blood boils before its final thickening
Before it is left to cool in Corinth, in Enterprise?
Young yeoman, rude in your blue eyes,
Straw hat cocked in the county's latest style
Was it defense, not wanting to miss the big event,
Or just being shy about staying home?
No matter. You walked to Corinth. You went.

Well, not being cavalry because you had no horse
Means nothing to us now who conjure your ghost.
We have been mostly the infantrymen
Of the country's armies—Hill 209, Hill 800.
Yes sir, they have numbers.
We feel the earth as we walk to the world's wars,
And remembering, we return to care again,

57

Planting the seeds to tide us until the next
Rearing of the Apocalyptic face.

In the middle of May you found yourself
Not only in Company A, but in Polk's First Corp.
You also found what enlisted men know—
Being scared is only half.
There was typhoid, measles, and dysentery;
Also nothing to eat.
Instead of the clear water of the Chickasawhay
Here muddy, stagnant holes
Held what there was to drink.
How you soldiered and how you died
We don't know. Diaries tell us
What days it rained. We know Polk's Corp
Was beyond the entrenchments skirmishing day and night.
Everyone prepared for the coming fight.

As always the enlisted men were the last to know—
All units would fall back to Tupelo.
Perhaps this was your last bright sight
As the torches were put
To the trunks and tents, the blankets and beds,
As eighteen thousand in hospitals moved
Farther south.
No great battle, just plenty dead.

Grandfather, as you leaked away in June
Did you think at all of generation?
Your wife even then carried a son.
Did dreaming take its hands and urge you
Past Corinth to her labor to come,

To us, unnumbered, unknown
But coming, grandfather . . . coming.
Your blood may have thickened in Corinth
Yet your seed twisted to a birthing scream,
Your blood surged to now,
Surges like a sea in my head
Even as it may have spoken to you lying there
In your cocked hat,
Now tipped to shade your eyes, now tipped to die.

What now for the unknown soldier?
Somewhere in this plot of four hundred Confederates
Your bones stopped
But your blood salts leached the ground
On their way to the Chunky and Okatibbe,
On down the Chickasawhay, past the summer corn,
And the homestead you left unfinished,
On to larger holdings. Your salt blood
Moved now down the Pascagoula,
Out to the Gulf of Mexico, out to the salt seas
Embracing the earth, holding us all.
Your home is large now, your wraith has a name.
You rest in your sons
Who must keep you to keep themselves.